Contents

Matthew's grandad gave him some money.

Here's £2 for you.

Thank you!

My Money

Paul Humphrey

Photography by Chris Fairclough

W

First published in 2005 by
Franklin Watts
96 Leonard Street
London EC2A 4XD

Franklin Watts Australia
Level 17/207 Kent Street
Sydney NSW 2000

© 2005 Franklin Watts

ISBN 0 7496 6179 8 (hbk)
ISBN 0 7496 6191 7 (pbk)

Dewey classification number: 332.4

A CIP catalogue record for this book is available
from the British Library.

Planning and production by Discovery Books Limited
Editor: Rachel Tisdale
Designer: Ian Winton
Photography: Chris Fairclough
Series advisors: Diana Bentley MA and Dee Reid MA,
Fellows of Oxford Brookes University

The author, packager and publisher would like to thank the following
people for their participation in this book: Arrandeep and Suki Bola,
Ottilie and Penny Austin-Baker, Matthew and Julie Morris and family,
W & C. A. Griffiths garage, Leintwardine, W. H. Smith, Woolworths.

Printed in China

11

To Ottilie

have a **great time!**

Happy Birthday
love from
Auntie Laura & family
x x x

happy birthday

Ottilie got
£5 for her
birthday.

Arran has saved £15 - a ten pound note and five coins.

Sir Arran
the knight.

23

Word bank

Look back for these words and pictures.

Book

Change

Coins

Electric car

Game

Money

Note

Paints

Saved